PRAISE FOR
CHAOS INSIDE THUNDERSTORMS

— "There is no hint of apology or a waver of doubt in what he knows, and what he knows he makes available with a sense of responsibility. There is a deep sense of community within his poetry and it is this quality that transcends Garry and his writing beyond a limiting definition of male or poetry or Indigenous. His (literary) voice resonates like music. The ways of the old ones vibrate from within the writing without romantic nuance but with forthright presence. We are all fortunate to learn from Garry as a mature writer who has travelled an individual road measured with experience resulting in a high form of literary practice."

—JANET ROGERS, Mohawk & Victoria's Poet Laureate

— "My aunt Aimee George has a saying for our men: 'Warrior up.' Garry's words must have floated on the winds to her as he sat and composed this amazing set of poems. The poetry is about warrioring up. Out of the 'rotting silence' emerges a new history, poetic, powerful and poignant. Fearless in the making, Garry again emerges as one of the most beautiful voices in Indigenous country, pushing against the propaganda of the church, the state and its educators in lyric poems that inspire us to pick up our bundles and push back too."

—LEE MARACLE, author of *Ravensong*

— "If irony can be useful to 'rage,' then Garry Gottfriedson shows how in *Chaos Inside Thunderstorms*. He uses the word 'thunderstorm' in a love poem, but passion is also part of his rage against the pains and injustices of colonization. These poems are shaped against the havoc of the conqueror's spoils and spoiling, the 'dogs' let loose in an anger that must resonate with all of us. His words remind us that 'No More' is also a Growl!"

—FRED WAH, Canada's Parliamentary Poet Laureate

— "*Chaos Inside Thunderstorms* is a dream of prayers laced with light and hope. I loved it. All of it. This is Garry Gottfriedson at his finest."

—RICHARD VAN CAMP, author of *The Lesser Blessed*

CHAOS INSIDE
thunderstorms

OTHER BOOKS BY
GARRY GOTTFRIEDSON

100 Years of Contact (1990)

In Honour of Our Grandmothers (1994)

Glass Tepee (2002)

Painted Pony (2005)

Whiskey Bullets (2006)

Skin Like Mine (2010)

Jimmy Tames Horses (2012)

Deaf Heaven (2016)

Clinging to Bone (2019)

CHAOS INSIDE
thunderstorms

GARRY GOTTFRIEDSON

RONSDALE

CHAOS INSIDE THUNDERSTORMS
Copyright © 2014 Garry Gottfriedson
Second Printing February 2023

RONSDALE PRESS
3350 West 21st Avenue, Vancouver, B.C., Canada V6S 1G7
www.ronsdalepress.com

Typesetting: Julie Cochrane, in New Baskerville 11 pt on 13.5
Cover Design: Julie Cochrane
Cover Art: Tania Willard, Red Willow Designs

Ronsdale Press wishes to thank the following for their support of its publishing
program: the Canada Council for the Arts, the Government of Canada through
the Canada Book Fund, the British Columbia Arts Council, and the Province
of British Columbia through the Book Publishing Tax Credit Program.

Library and Archives Canada Cataloguing in Publication

Gottfriedson, Garry, 1954–, author
    Chaos inside thunderstorms / Garry Gottfriedson.

Poems.
Issued in print and electronic formats.
ISBN 978-1-55380-326-3 (print)
ISBN 978-1-55380-328-7 (ebook) / ISBN 978-1-55380-327-0 (pdf)

    I. Title.

PS8563.O8388C43 2014   C811'.6   C2014-900055-3   C2014-900056-1

At Ronsdale Press we are committed to protecting the environment. To this
end we are working with Canopy and printers to phase out our use of paper
produced from ancient forests. This book is one step towards that goal.

Printed in Canada.

To the Secwepemc women activists
fighting against the destruction of
our land, air and water

&

in honour of Dr. Janice Dick-Billy,
Kanahus Manuel, Maranda Dick
and Pam Richard —

My grandchildren are in your hands

CONTENTS

– chaos –

– inside –

– thunderstorms –

— chaos —

In the Forest

peace turned up loudly
for a moment
with boisterous clomping on forest floors
allegro on pathways over twigs
serenading butterflies with the blues
ears perked dog-like
straining for the chirp of birds
telescope eyes scanned bushes
on the lookout for bears stuffing their bellies
full of raspberries and strawberries
lulling spirit songs
out of honour
in respect because of pity

and then the forest falls
chainsaws and machines rip heavy metal music
trees drop
turn to planks
butterflies flee
die screaming
Chicken Little drops from the sky
worms surface as evergreens fall
mountainsides slide into the river
salmon float belly up
black bears scavenge garbage bins
knee-bent tourists rummage the debris
click, click their cameras
believe they are one with the wild
until they are eaten alive

Google can't help anymore
GPS has a virus
there is no safe place on sea or land or in the sky
labourers scream for solace
drop their faces onto their oil-layered hands
shame is the sound of money exported
angst is for the love of your company

peace dies of cancer

Tk'emlu'ps

inside the brown of skin
sounds never die
a river alive swirls bone
setétkwe — the rapid waters flow
over membrane and within muscle
then lap the tip of the tongue
telling the eyes
melpétkwe — look at my reflection
souls are at the edge of skin
stuttering old river songs
serenading the deaf
owl-dancing with the crippled
calling the impaired to limp
backwards into the vortex

inside the brown of skin
the mind never rests
river songs create new meaning
when the skin is drunk
the tongue wags dysfunction
for the throat is dry love
suicide is lateral violence
puffing on a beaten-down chest
coiled in a fist of words
that can never be taken back
impaling another's soul
and when the dirty work has been done
a crooked, black smile shines
victory
and the rez thrives, the rivers surge

inside the brown of skin
sounds never die

Tk'emlu'ps: the Secwepemc name for Kamloops

High Priests

from the hard corners in my head
I see the cardinals of sin
eating godliness on the red carpets
quilting the streets in the city of angels

I fled to Colorado one thing in mind
I wanted to coward crawl into your soul
cling to you reckless
but then I saw Ginsberg's eyes undressing me

dizzy in my own desperation
I knew Colorado was not for me
the eyes within the Rockies followed me west
and I crumpled the mirrors cupped in my fists

because the face that moved across the mirror was mine
seeking out assassins who medicate cowards
sleeping in LA's streets with beggars and prostitutes
there again, I saw your face in that crowd, your ghost

it began to bend my body into shadows
as I listened to skins bursting on the streets
razors scraped across my forehead
my head was full of the living marching to death camps

I scrawled their names across my back like swastikas
memory revived through my limbs
my vulture eyes scanned the skeletons and corpses
and scavenged stars in funeral processions tromping to LA's
                                          catacombs

and my mouth foamed
so that I became drunk on my own spit
while their words bearing split-tongue hisses
crawled into my ears, Michael Jackson's ears, Stephen
                                        Harper's ears

my face bloated
my jaw ached
my tongue bled poems
my logic crouched in black corners

I realized in the darkness of misunderstandings
they were born to drop to their knees
clawing and tugging at Christian Dior hems
sucking on cocks of dead men outstretched in morgues

there, the undertakers in white coats count the cash
even before the guts are dropped into stainless steel buckets
filling their mouths with sins, disinfecting bodies
embalming them with formaldehyde

they lie stiff on steel beds, faces softened to prettiness
anal cavities and vaginas stuffed with gauze
ready to hide from life as we know it
this is when they ride Harleys all the way to heaven

and at the gates, *On the Road* Kerouac flashed across my mind
my tears pleaded with him to take Ginsberg home
to burn the red carpets in Hollywood
to awaken me as *Howl* once did

and when I forced myself to look away from the mirror
I cleared my head of regrets
forgave them, all of them
and now I sleep in peace

in peace

Idle No More

and what poetry
would Duncan Campbell Scott write
of Chief Theresa Spence?

his words are dead
and have died many lives
in the hearts of other Canadians

all of them meant to live
and destroy
the very essence of aboriginality

December 21, 2012, solstice, a holy day
the day Stephen Harper smudged
himself with rhetoric, laid it down on the dotted line

the day of oligarchic triumph
but for whom?
the colonial handover can never be

Idle No More is a time
to unknot all inhibitions
tangled in the hair of a silenced people

to kill Bill C-45 is not murder
it is what Goya did
when he painted revolutions

it is the will of a hero
a spirit who refuses
an abortion of tribal rights

and so she offers
her life
for the land, the people, all people

Chief Theresa Spence, let it be known —
D.C. Scott has no poetry to write of you
but I do

Rendered Natural

eradication began
with Pope Alexander VI in 1493

divine will
turned acts of piracy into charters and patents

the pope and monarchs laid
the groundwork for colonial extermination

of seventy-two million North American Natives
genocide deepened the pope's love

canonical jurisprudence was the duty
that transformed "savages" into copyrights

butchery and resource confiscation were the first
patents rendered natural

Eurocentric notions framed piracy
and drove their impulses

labour intensified
theft is legitimized capitalism

since Monsanto has replaced the prince
the goal is to discover, conquer and own the souls of
indigenous folk

the duty to Christianize is now interchanged
with the duty to commercialize

thus, the second coming of Columbus is entrenched
with the utilization of biotechnologies

the gift is no longer a few beads, pots and smallpox
but cancer, the mass sterilization of women, and now men

the theft of children in the name of
civilization was the crown

it is the gift of poverty
the bright lights of skid row

the men who drive by seeking
whores in their own mothers

the penitentiaries stuffed full of
indigenous men, women and children

the barbwire that proves
Indians are truly captured

it is the Harpers, the presidents and popes of the world
who anxiously pimp their citizens

in the name of economics
unchanged since 1493

Chaos

in a time when there is deep-rooted chaos
roiling in this country,
where are the voices of our chiefs?

Trudeau's 1969 White Paper was defeated
when all chiefs in Canada stood
together in solidarity

unison is not about the entrapments
of grandstanding, more tax laws, and economic development
the platform of the day

it is about standing together
to take coup in a new era of colonialism
where foreigners are on the take

because of mining
because of the continuation of expropriation
because of Harper's government

ENOUGH!

Dogs of War

enter the war zone
let the dogs out

initiate the troops
let the dogs howl

call all generals
let the dogs whiff

prepare for death
let the dogs taste blood

strategize for control
let the dogs drink

stand your ground
let the dogs slobber

blow up the mines
let the dogs burn

slay the enemy
let the dogs eat meat

punish the horrified
let the dogs digest

gather the fallen
let the dogs regurgitate

never admit defeat
let the dogs fuck

Deaf Heaven

Canada's pathetic apology
shoved down the throat

force-feeding
a truth and reconciliation cure

words used before
heaved in places that shouldn't have been

acts of contrition, a replacement
for virtue and rape

no chief can mend tyranny
if the vision is not theirs

as *our fathers* and *holy water* is not a strong-
enough plea for deliverance

nor wish dead men walking
on earth into a deaf heaven

the boys get away again
hide in cloud nine

implore prayers for themselves
and drip, drip, drip dirty decades later

so Canada, what part of the bible washes away that sin?

Residential Schools

residential schools raised generations
of misogynists and misandrists
the pedagogy of hate nurtured 'til death do us part

racist policy tattooed in the brain
delivering civilization and assimilation
the subtle pedagogy of civilized leadership

and those who followed the natural law
became dizzy-sick with chaotic guilt
because what the holy men delivered was unnatural

this is when the pretty girls became toothless
and the tough boys became women
and the self-assured beaten down in shades of violet

it became a history of putrid self-loathing
sending weakened warriors to vasectomies
filling courtrooms with endorsements of hung-over shame

this is the androgyny of the enlightened

There Are No Chiefs Anymore

for Vera Manuel and all women who have taken a stand

my mind cannot rest
I spend sleepless nights
ripping apart destruction
ripping apart pain
ripping apart genocide
in Indian country

in Indian country
picket-fenced wrecks of rusted one-eyed Fords
and no-wheel Chevys corral government Indians
bootleg papas and crack-sell'n mamas make do
between makeshift welfare programs and shipments of goods

in Indian country
metro-sexual Indian agents shake hands
with skinny-legged pot-bellied men
who believe they have purpose
the deal done
their fate doomed

in Indian country
half-educated yappers fly high at the mouth
long time professional students flamingo step tight-assed
into the secret rooms on Parliament Hill with dogmatic
diplomacy
they remind their audience
of Wounded Knee
of Oka
but no one mentions The Highway of Tears
the numbers of Aboriginal women who disappeared

turned up dead
and nothing gets done

our reserves are firetraps
hazard-waste incinerators
incest-infected paradises
and havens for Indian experts

where have our chiefs gone?
N'kwala
Smallboy
Manuel
where are you?
come back to us
you were winners
you were leaders
you were chiefs

in Indian country
I am ghost-walker
trudging in thick fog
that lingers — never gives
that lingers — never rises
that lingers — never leaves

like the broken halos of fallen angels
a wretched thing given to hobby Indian chiefs
prostituting
their children
their mothers
their grandmothers
and my home

in Indian country
we don't have chiefs anymore
but puppet, barrel-fat mis-chiefs
chicken-dancing for white women

parading Pocahontas Barbie dolls in grand entries
ridiculing the origins of their own births
scorning the life-givers of their own children
it has nothing to do with love
and everything with prestige
and now our pale-skinned wannabe Indian gals
lead their pony-tailed phonies
into sour Canadian dreams
that lock the jaws
into the edge of dictatorship
another form of expropriation
". . . sign on the dotted line"
she convinced him
with her legs spread
brown
white
beige
half-breeds — no breeds
dominate white paper policies

self government is no government
there are no lands set aside
for the use of Indians, Indians . . . Indians
how could it be?
how could it be?

in Indian country
the extermination policy constantly erupts
from green-eyed, round-bellied men
who dare call themselves "chief"
another cheap surprise

more ice filling the veins
to stop us from reproducing

more sharp nails prying apart eyelids
to keep sleep from entering

more scratching on chalkboards
to send begging ears to the mercy of down-filled pillows

more to drive the mind
into machine-gun madness

more
more
more

no more!

in Indian country
this is not about me

it is about a healthy past
it is about a healthy present
it is about a healthy future

where flowers will grow in the dark
for blind children

but can they burn the truth into the eyes of the innocent?
can they burn the truth past the walls of my brown skin?
can they burn love into these lips
and tell me they love a man
. who hates the power of genocide?

can they hold me on dark nights
and allow me to trust my manhood
along the bloodstained walls
where a different life began
and then fell into the plastic hands of strangers
and emerged into inherited chaos?

I will not bring a child into this world to kiss suicide
I will not touch pink lying lips
I will not protect century-old greed

the greed they lie for
the greed they protect
the greed they so dearly love

and I will no longer stand in silence
while genocide seductively sucks
the last remains from Indian country

we are the fixers of genocide

Activism

and so the poet is a targeted muse
for speaking poetically or otherwise
against colonial brainwashing

the intensity of ghettoized politics
should have died by now
with the honing of five decades of civil-rights activism

at the forefront of seven generations of name-calling
there are many who have stood their ground
for me and my grandchildren and they have died trying

hear the names of the dead
etched in Indian memory

Elijah Harper, Andrew Paul, Simon Baker, Chief Dan George,
George Manuel, Chief Robert Smallboy, Frank Calder, Richard
Malloway, Senator Guy Williams, Ed Sparrow, Joe Gosnell,
Chief Basil David, James Gladstone, Harry Daniels, Harold
Cardinal, Jim Sinclair, Howard Adams, Gordon Antione, Gus
Gottfriedsen, Joe Michel, and so many more in this country

Mildred Gottfriedson, Jane Gottfriedson, Vera Manuel,
Marceline Manuel, Dr. Mary Thomas, Margaret Leonard,
Genevive Muscle, Pauline Johnson, Mourning Dove, Irene
Billy, Anna Mae Aquash, Mary Two Axe Early, Mary John,
Gertie Guerin, and so many more in this country

Starkly Reverberated

cultural imperialism serves
to colonize and crush indigenous thought
before extinction is achieved

its factory is named assimilation
its mission is to annihilate
and it works like this

indigenous spirituality is the target commodity
seized and sold on the market by plastic medicine men
who vend the spirits before annihilation

the New Agers are the salesmen
trained in exploitation and expropriation
by way of books and needy elders   .

like scientists armed with scholarly declarations of war
ordained by politically correct gods
devoted strictly to claiming the indigenous voice

and who are mandated by the government and church
to do so righteously and swiftly
the New Agers are softly relentless

both scientists and New Agers pursue
the repackaging of indigenous thought
and wholesale it with supremacy zeal

the retail value is immense
peddled through government bills
flogged by holy men and bookstores worldwide

thus, white oppression perpetuates
ideological subordination
starkly reverberated

and it drives
economic, political and religious authorities to
raise a bastard child, named cultural imperialism

From Columbus to Monsanto

there are words for legal theft
like *terra nullius*
"property of the enemy
belonging to no one
and open for the taking"

the pope's policy was this:
take over the land and the people
authorize hysterectomies
sterilize indigenous cultures
become rich over indigenous bones

cardinal thoughts deem others inferior
as legalized theft is a western construct
stuffing the capitalist's mind full of cagey jargon
for the church
for the government
for the scientists
from an act of god

Columbus squirmed out from his coffin
and renamed himself Monsanto
the larva that spewed the maggot
the flies that ate women's carcasses
the cancers that killed men
the ghosts that drove children mad

like Mengele, Columbus and Monsanto scientifically approved
the manipulation of life forms
that science is a new religion called "greed"
it crawled out of their heart caskets
and into minds that envisioned eternal take-over

the coronation of twins is expressed through patenting
a technique of dominance
a hybrid of genetically modified genomes
a construct of legalizing piracy
a writ hand-signed by monarchs, popes, presidents and CEOs

indigenous people know
that guns and cannons are now replaced with needles
and that business is owning a piece of nature
for the church
for the government
for the scientists
for the rich

terra nullius hides in the Jekyll and Hyde of man
clawing at the stitches
that bind their corpses
living in memory
as each country positions for dominance
making up the rules
for the evolution of greed
and finally, stomping on those with homelands

Mining and War

in a world gone soft
dogs bark on October nights
no self-respecting man can warm his hands
as a cold-hearted corporate prisoner

the spine in our country labours
as the land is eaten alive
no one hears
the sounds of a mother mourning

but indigenous folk do
who are the root-diggers
who are the berry pickers
who are the hunters
who are the horsemen
who are the fishermen
who are the pharmacists
who are the healers

who never walk the streets phone to ear
but know emotional and spiritual security
streams from the silence of earth
and that wars are waged against our Mother

those who become prime ministers
those who become presidents
those who become corporation fiends
those who become murderous millionaires
those who become societal slaves
those who become the merchants of blood
those who become tragically greedy

believe in ink and rage
when the dogs bark at night
sending a flurry of death warrants
thinking war is a luxury afraid to be missed
thinking they must get to work
in a world gone soft

English

since Indians have learned
to speak English, we have blamed
the white man for every screw-up
and Turtle Island has never been the same

using the Queen's nouns and verbs
was our brilliant tragedy
a historical poem to chew salad by
whites and reds tossed by chance

it was a fine line in motherhood
teaching children to speak
with civilized tongues in residential schools
giving history new meaning

wrapping our vocal cords
around foreign languages
avoiding responsibility at all cost
and so, blaming others for our mistakes was easy

the clock has no pity
time has taught us to read things well
Napoleon was right when he said
"History is a set of [white] lies to be agreed upon"

Ceremonial Humiliation

a meeting or a funeral?
that is the question
for sovereign to sovereign to answer

emotional intelligence means
there is a heart at risk
simply, she has it; he doesn't

it is a political mistake
playing ceremonial humiliation games
Canada is at stake

the voice of reasonable leadership
may cause the judges to twirl their chairs
to see who holds the best pitch

older folk judge and praise
with steadfastness but grow shy
when there is a gun aimed at their hearts

and Indians are well-defined hunter/gatherers
all it takes is Elijah Harper with a feather in hand
and a ceremony of their own

a prime minister's notion of "civilized" societies is convenient
for it renders neat legalisms as non-racist policy
that rolls across this land

what was he thinking?
he has broken all promises
even to his own children

Forgotten Soldiers

Canada, my country, I am yours
the forgotten soldier left behind
the lines of your broken treaties
to ensure my survival
and no more war with you

I am the dust of my people
I am the blood of my birth
I am the protector of both

I will not take up arms against you
but for you and my Mother
I spin prayers through my duties
to clear skies in sun dances
I talk to the Old Ones
and ask them to sail with me
over salt waters for you, Canada
I ask them to guard
my red blood on the same white shores
that carried Cartier and Cook to my ancestors

Canada, my country, I will forgive
your black guilt in honour of my Mother
and for my people
but understand that I am your forgotten soldier
muddled with the expectation of your dreams
where innocence dies at the speed of bullets
where shattered bones lie
in puddles of blameless blood

I am not your murderer
yet my prison is only brushed clean
when I have gathered enough courage
to embarrass you in a world of children

Canada, my country, my freedom is the entrapment
by your federal bureau files
stacked amid the layers
of your dirty legal work
yet you do not know me

you do not know
the stone-drunk world that I live in
nor the sweaty nightmares
of legs and limbs climbing out
of foxholes filled with corpses and mud

since you arrived, I fight my own spirit
throw rocks into rivers
hoping to change
the course of chronic war dreams
my mornings and nights are always the same
sharp edges like bayonets
slicing off layers of musky skin
my helmet full
of life after death
yet I swallow hard
and push myself to sit stiffly before the flame

bent forward, I draw heat
search in an endless dusk
smile from a stone perch
dream wide awake
dank of rain
that might have been a song of worship
travelling in the currents of my blood
and sung at a sun dance
or it could've been fine
European pottery crafted neatly
drawing me into another cell of death

Canada, my country, I am jerked
into the reality of war
once again piling junk sandbags
piecing them together like broken pottery
mending the mangled, motionless bodies
dead and scattered flowers blown apart
by the force of stone and gunpowder

tired, I rest and lie still
listen to the rain
fall on empty dreams
that die alone
on the ruined mountains leading to Paris
and when I escape in the mist and clouds
everywhere the war is wet
the earth tears itself open
it rears violently backwards
into the hearts of the brave
and I smother my ears
but still smell the bursting bodies
thickening the air
there are no more birds or animals or sun
only white ash fluttering to the earth like snow

my blood stops
my brain freezes
and finally, sleep creeps in
I disappear
into a deep dark hole

Canada, my country, I dream of home
watching red-tailed hawks
sail over snow blankets
searching for food
or dream I sit
by the wood stove
listening to the fire crackle
feasting on pemmican with Granny and Grandpa
or waltzing into the eyes of my sweetheart
until tears bring me back
to war

I awaken
and curse charcoal words at you, Canada
because your desire to liberate
concentration camps is your same desire
to imprison me on my return home

Canada, my country, you have overlooked
the bones of my brothers and sisters
scattered on foreign lands
how they have given their lives to save yours
you have forgotten
that I can never surrender my identity
even in the event of war
that your assimilation policies cannot turn me white

Canada, my country, you have turned
me into your forgotten soldier
have spat taunting lies at me
sentenced me
to live on skid row

Canada, my country, you have forgotten
I am a warrior
and the land belongs to me

Our Women

when the warriors vanished
so did purpose

it was then
Aboriginal women rose

fists coiled
in defence of those to whom they gave birth

grandmothers and mothers organized
to overthrow deception and genocide

Aboriginal women sought to
destroy culturally crippling policies

they are the elements
of natural power

they are the bridge
between earth to heaven

they laboured re-birth when
the opposition desired death

our women never wavered from
the love of their children, people and land

we have them to be thankful for
and so I am

Abandonment of the Essential Self

assimilation is the discourse to prostitution
and identity-marketing for mainstream citizenship
never translates to distinctiveness
it is colonization instead

dominant agreement means
"you give me everything — I give you nothing"
it is blatant dictatorship
without benefits

the essential self thus abandons Mother
denies uniqueness
shames the life-giver
becomes a dumping ground

there is no such thing as
"we are all the same, we are one, we are global"
for supremacy does not bargain colour
it is all or nothing white

The Indian Act

there is no white law accurate
enough to protect Indian rights

there is no white law accurate
enough to corral Indians

there is no white law accurate
enough to slice the Indian tongue

there is no white law accurate
enough to split the retina

there is no white law accurate
enough to deafen the ears

there is no white law accurate
enough to rip the heart out

there is no white law accurate
enough to stop salmon from running

there is no white law accurate
enough to stunt forest growth

there is no white law accurate
enough to mine the Earth empty

there is no white law accurate
enough to deny Natural Law

Because

because of what we have become
we lick salt-soaked asphalt
protesting causes that ignite
drums and songs in our throats

because a colossus of eyes rhythmically
cheers champions on
and beats down losers
victory songs boom on city streets

because we are born as protestors
we battle corporations like Nu Gold, Ajax and so on
stand our ground against the Canadian Gestapo
and know that roots are indigenous to land

because we can taste the iodine
within our blood
when we near solidarity
we are Indians once again

because our ears corral
the sound of our hearts breaking
when one more son or daughter falls
our tears flow at the grave

because our intuition is alive
movements come forth
sharpen our knowledge
lead us to understanding

because life is about living
and death is about memory
respect drums beneath our skins
calling on holy songs for the love of this land

because our souls can withstand
more than we undergo
but less than we want to
trust is higher than ourselves

just because . . .

Open Sights

I am crazy
vowels grumbling off my tongue
writing of whimsical turmoil
blending consonants that weave a rutting song

I am dangerous in autumn
fine-tuned by the crispness of air
scraping horns on aspens
grunting near sweet springs and salt licks

I am weird in transition
searching the oncoming winter
hearing the hunter's heart
smelling the sweat on the trigger

I am the open sights
the crossroads that wait ahead
knowing that it is not about death
but the ecstasy of living

Theresa and Stephen

PART 1: THERESA

Stephen, "hear my heart's staunch call"
islands of my people, my blood, my victory
awaken to your Victorian rasp
reservations bleed
stems and roots drain the last of life
the indigenous land will forever be parched
if you get your way

yet from this wintery season to eternity
the natural world takes action
snow builds
layers of prayers
in this month, the month of Christ's birth
I am not alone
in your rotting silence

hear what I have to say:
the land is alive
I sit amid ancestors
compelled to obey
my Creator's pull towards heaven
my forebears
fought for this land
and because of them
I am here
and I stand as they once did

"I will die for my land, my people"
although you may not remember me
from the days of Attawapiskat
mine is an old voice
which you cannot understand
the vowels rumbling in my throat
tell the story of indigenous people everywhere
words and then actions weave
through the land
the songs and dances that spring
from the marrow of my brothers and sisters
is the beating heart of Mothers, the life-givers
the packers of culture
nothing is idle no more
for these are the sounds
of earth, of mountains, of streams
of prairie, of tundra, of Canada
the lakes and rivers swirling
with the birth of our origins
the same ones that Duncan, himself, had written about

like him, you loathe the origins of our births
yet you fantasize the existence of our being
the waters in which my children tumble
the flowers of which I speak

all I ask is that you give
what Canada has promised
and destroy the promise
you made of selling the skin, blood, marrow
of this great country
I call home
you call home

unblock the greed
barricading your ears
listen to me, Stephen
the bills you concoct in parliament
will not make Canada wealthier
the constitutional sections you wish to dissolve
will be your ultimate demise

are you willing
to go down in history
for treason
as Canada's executioner?

I do not beg you
there is no word
in my mother tongue for begging
so I ask you to bring
the man within you forward
to sit before me, a warrior woman
sipping on the broth of animals
to speak of unbroken treaties
laws since time began
to count the sun's return
as long as the sun shines
as long as the grass grows
as long as the rivers flow
this was written in Red Rock and on paper

I have planted my language
my prayer on this island
across from you, your 24-Sussex-Drive mansion
your parliament, your walls and your corners
in your head full of ghosts
driving you mad, Stephen
do I dare say your name?

I whispered it
"IDLE NO MORE"
and the meaning, its intent
shot across this country
a tidal wave of action flooded this world
carried the soft rumbling of mouth sounds
faster than the fire that boils
your hatred for me

because the grannies who reached
into my bones are infinite
and they sit with me in this tepee

so strange, you do not know
that your lineage stops with you
and that your hatred is my bliss
your ego will not allow you to
die an embarrassing death
but your stubbornness is my great advantage

eyes are everywhere, Stephen
watching your fear
of old women swelling
your tongue with dirty words
behind your face
full of make-up
in the hours when spirits call
the names of my ancestors
you seek the racist advice
of men five generations old attuned
and shaken by the same distress
they do not have the answers
like you, they are the oxen and plough
and voice of redneck Canada
a minority so rotten
they prostituted their own mothers

and now they are dead
sounds tumbling like weeds across this land
stinging the ears of my brothers and sisters
ricocheting off the drums pounding Round-Dance songs
and the web circles the earth
bringing forth those
to announce to Canada
"you are liars"
"you are hypocrites"

do not fear me, Stephen
I am not the enemy

PART 2: STEPHEN

it is beyond me
to hear your words
to say your name
to call you Chief
to even be in the presence
of your living flesh

it is not polite
to publicly speak of you
the woman who causes
the grinding of my teeth
the sweat between my legs

I am the eye of Canada
I am the most photographed prime minister
loved by the people
even my hairdresser knows this
but it is our secret
public figures do not declare anything
but I profess to you

I am not the problem
you are!

Theresa, I will tell you this
although your people may see me
as spiritless and cunning
my acquisition of personal wealth
is an example of where I can take Canada
I have new names
with dollar signs in my retina
a new face for the dollar bill
all for this country
all for my people
all for me

despite your nuisance protests
I will plough the earth with massive pipelines
bleeding out the oil
with the hands
of Asian imports
as did my predecessor, John A. Macdonald
building Canada's railway sea-to sea

my hands will cramp
digging through archives
to find a way to splendour
and with the sale of Canada
I will bend and alter Canadian law to do so
do not stand in my way, Woman Warrior Chief
for the white man's law overpowers your Creator

do not take this as a threat
there is no need for me
to make idle threats
I am absolute law
above God and glory

my silence is my weapon — your enemy
I call war against you
against your people
against those who stand with you

and the war has just begun
it will have a lasting
impact on Aboriginal cultures
for another 150 years
overshadowing previous accounts of Canadian history
there will be not one Indian alive
to relive, to retell this war
I am about to wage

instinctively I know you are near heaven
but I want you in hell
even in my sleep
I dream
dream of you spooning my back
the old cougar you are
cunning and prowling
having your way with me — the head of Canada!

I cannot recover
the occasion after it is missed
just as I cannot recover
the stone after it is thrown
the time after it is gone
the word after I have spoken it

so, I remind you
we have no history of colonialism
Canada is big enough to make a difference
but not big enough to threaten anybody
it is a huge asset if properly used

finally, Theresa
never forget
never forget
never forget
I am not the problem
you are

– inside –

Inside

inside churches and jails
rape-rotted rosaries
stitched crucifixes to skin
threaded prayers to palms
tongues dreaded being caught in lies
outside on the streets

and the poets said nothing
as saxophones and barbeques guided their discussions
there were daisies and cute things to write about
instead of doing their job
and it was all tasteless
pretentious behavior

and in the back alleys innocence is god's word
spat out by priests, nuns and other holy men
who licked pussies
who fucked boys
who prayed for redemption

and the poets said nothing
but grooved to saxophones and ate red meat on Friday
licked their lips in philosophical fear
pretended that poetry was only for the rich
who stuck to themselves

but god's doors, prison doors, clanked shut
the keys stuffed into the cleavages of salvation
and the disillusioned prisoners lay on beds
dreamed they were the pussy-eaters
fucking themselves with rosaries in hand

and the poet finally said
reconciliation is another cash-cow lie
growing in the belly of the elite
holy and dark

Questions

hating yourself is the greatest
love of all

I remember the taste
tingling on my tongue

I have heard the melody
of this ecstasy vibrating in my bones

I sang in harmonic bliss
accentuating the dead still fresh in sound

my mother, my grandmothers, my dead lovers
all ash, all dust, all for me to grieve

I scribbled poems until my wrists hurt
then again, I questioned my writing, my words, my words

. . . all ash, ash . . . all dust, dust . . . all grieving, grieving
pieces of the ones gone . . . my matriarchs, my loves

eternally flutter within
sonnets vomiting ink

I published them all, all of them
in capitalistic greedy print

and when the ink became
cracked black islands like desert floors

I yelled, I screamed, I warned my grandsons
who skated away with angels

gone to sacred places, never to return
disgusted with reality

tormenting their souls
they hid in the shadows of heaven

they shouted back
"you are a fool"

understanding is something else
respect is expected

yet the bombs still dropped from heaven
dangerous things burst out of the ordeal

I spat vile words
ran for water to dilute the dry ink

and the rest of the country braced for the aftershock
because the muddy roads filled with women's blood

I scribbled more poems
Goya was my manic pen

because of their screams
because of their love for me

because there was no projector for this film
because I was Goya alive

no film previewed
no dogs barked

no audience
no sound

no gawking eyes
no evidence

that someone hated himself
enough to cause terror

that someone forgot
sacredness

that someone made love
by the tombstones of war

and now, orphans drink from gutters
shake their fists towards god

watch their mothers disappear
become deaf from their fathers' outrage

who said they could bomb
their way into a feminist paradise

who said they could create
sounds for hearing-impaired sons of macho men

and once the bodies dissolved to dust
the birds still sang somewhere else

it was a garden of birds
where musicians were forbidden to play

but hoped someone heard the notes
the story, the story, the story of my self hate

tell it like it is. hear me?
hear me? tell it like it is

news. news flashes from around the world
it is my story

Taliban of a different sort
get the results

desire little hotties in black dresses
become predators to orphan boys

take pride in the ashes of their loved ones
flying lost in glory, and then

stomping their way to earth
detonating rage when they land

it is so far from life
it is psychological spiritualism

dancing backwards
leading souls into the land of milk and honey

there, Holocaust was a word
before it was born

a holy land full of dread
the devout pitted in an abyss

it is what I keep my grandchildren from
it is what I was given

only now, I realize
that utopia is the love you give yourself

When I Was an Indian

when I was an Indian
I should've died

my hair blond
I might've been a cowboy

times were good then

Crows and Back Alleys

watch for the crows
in Vancouver's back alleys
where at nightfall the scavengers wait
for weakness to drop

peccadilloes swing from hides there
gravity draws dreams to the grave
they grunt, blow steam for staying power
and test the witness' will to live

god has isolated them
the diocese made their stand known
between Gastown and Chinatown on the damp asphalt
the congregation buzzes meth hand to mouth

back out on Robson Strasse
sushi and Christmas pervade the air
in December the rain halts briefly for Jesus
enough time for trendy side-steppers to cross

well-to-do foreigners tippy-toe in Gucci heels
bypass gelato and Cuban cigar bars on the way to Thurlow
Street
another siren breaks the pitter-pattering of feet
shuffling along to get a fix of caffeine and raw fish

Jim Morrison wrote about these things somewhere else
long before now-a-days' poets discovered daisies to write about
the back alleys on Vancouver's East Side are still the same
and the crows haven't changed much either

Infinite

cruising the notorious other self takes
a guy into the hideous ghetto within

since in every corner of his body lurks
another astonishing guy he never knew

there are countless men whose bodies swell
with self loathing

like Willie Pickton full of himself
indulging in remorseless narcissism

standing in front of a mirror
pulling lipstick out of his shirt pocket

painting dirty things on mirrors
spelling out the terrifying "pig" within

staring into the eyes of victims
before they were devoured in the hog trough

they have names
all of them: Leigh, Laura, Maria, Cindy . . . gone . . . gone

so when the boars grunted with full bellies
the police officers perked up

to drag their lame asses to cruise the East Side
immune to beaten-down women raging "motherfucker killer'

the law-scorned daughters, sisters and mothers
laughed on the record, for the record

and when the secret slut prowling within the uniform was
                                        unleashed
public queries became the trash that set fire to the streets

holy men from all nations calling on God
to end this apocalypse

families of the victims yanked out the last strands of hair
graying on their heads full of their daughters' memories

knowing the police had an addiction of their own
called apathy

because Pickton's psychopathic love
over-ruled logic again and again

teams of reinforcement reinforced deviant behavior
of both Willie and the police

let the mothers and fathers and sisters and brothers
of Pickton's victims shred him into the slop he is

let solidarity fume within the marrow of loved ones
so that the Picktons and Dahmers and Bundys burn at the stake

take to the streets in remembrance of the East Side women
and those strewn along the Highway of Tears

hold tight the child whose mother is slaughtered memory
dry the rust that drips from the orphan's eyes

finally, rejoice that we are alive as witness
and because of them we move, we scream resolution

they are infinite
we are infinite

A Dream Poem

in a house made of knives
carcasses hang from the walls

reservation glass is scattered across the floor
while the special ones sleep

the taste of burnt meat
still lingering on their palates

Indian babes slumber
dream of a Secwepemc knife song

the razor blade melody lulls
a death warrant track

the acoustics are powerful
the notes stick to shattered windows

red and jagged reflections of the dead
scatter in recollected history

dull shades of early morning
seep through the curtains as song birds sing

awakening the sweetness
that all dreams die sooner or later

When You Forget

it's when you forget
the warmth of the comforter
the mornings you crawled out of bed
during winter

it's when you forget
the soles of your feet
walked on hardwood floors
to stoke the family's fire that morning

it's when you forget
the aroma of coffee brewing
when you stepped out of the shower
and made your way to the beginning of day

it's when you forget
the colour of a winter morning
and the sound of the snow's heart breaking
beneath your feet

it's when you forget
the taste of your partner's lips
as you rode that roller coaster
from passion and fury to the calmness that followed

it's when you forget
the scent of your lover's natural musk
while you made love last
and didn't want it to end

it's when you forget
you discovered the meaning of love
as you lay your first born on your chest
the moment you became a parent

it's when you forget
the bond between parent and child
and you knew the struggles
as they strolled onwards

it's when you forget
that life is about living
and death is always a step away
unchangeable

it's when you forget
there are people in this world
who needed you
who depended on you

it's when you forget
people will be left behind
never understanding your decisions
but forced to live with them

it's when you forget
and you pulled that trigger
or climbed into that rope
never to return

it's when you forget
that it is we who will carry
that anger
that pain

that burden

The Death of a Hero

I am at a loss
for meaning
and metaphor

I had elevated you
to heaven
above all and everything

only to realize
it is exciting
to witness the death of a hero

This Death Is Different

there is grinding in our guts
as we dig the grave once again
for another clan member
who has fallen

this death is different.

it is anger churning
out questions
that can never be answered
until our time is up

this death is different.

it is silent betrayal
ditches of tears
gun powder in the eyes
dryly staring at the casket

this death is different.

because compassion is
sand in the mouth
mercury in the blood
razors in the palm of the hand

this death is different.

no one knows
if you should be cursed at
or loved in this moment
of total bewilderment

this death is different.

for we will witness
the children you bore
drop to their knees at the bone yard
begging God for enlightenment

this death is different.

there will be no angels sounding trumpets
marching your soul to heaven
when the last shovel of dirt is dropped
on the memories we bury

this death is different

because you have made a fool of us
and humility is our gift
awkwardly acquired and blameless
now we are forced to stand strong

The Storyteller

for Richard Van Camp

there is no soul
older than the storyteller's

rich with the language of those gone
and burdened with the words
that must be spoken

their blood is alive with relatives
clawing their way to the surface of the tongue
scrambling in the writer's brain
with memories desperate to escape
onto the roadmaps of lined paper
and clogging pens with waiting words
and images fluttering for those too afraid
to tell tales of their own battles

the storyteller is relentless in
the pursuit of experience
that scrapes our skins
wounds our dignities or
rips our hearts open to love

he is a post-modern *Koyoti*
shape-shifting his way into our marrow
so that we never forget
we are alive

Dead Girls Talk

dead girls talk amid still aspens
drawing ears to secrets
causing brain blizzards

along the Highway of Tears
riddles feed tyrants
insidiously

dead girls talk tingles spines
churns guts hysterically
pukes a colonial battery

vulnerability
dizzy with nightmares
brings Canada's reality to life

dead girls talk pounds
determination into hope
reminding us that we are among the living

the talk of the day is of bones
wanting to return home
to rest

Cultural Norms

my culture is not a circus
the abstention from original thought

it is beyond mediocre thinking
expressions of ancestral aesthetics

sinew woven from generation to generation
people alive

too many see skimpily clad
women in Pocahontas costume

feather-bent Geronimos
fists cupped with beer mugs

two-spirited boys
on the hunt for George Custer

I'll never wear laughables for any man
strip naked for desperadoes to jazz

swing a tambourine from my hip at powwows
do an Argentine tango at a sweat lodge

place my tongue on sacred objects
moan earth chants at operas

crack open a tepee door in downtown Toronto
pretend I'm Lewis or Clark

I'll never bastardize another's culture
for the sake of a chimera

draw up cartoon posters
of aboriginal women

sculpt circumcised privates
of white men painted brown

exploit the origins
of their birthrights

my culture is tattooed
on my body

the icons of my people prominently
inked for life

imprinted wrinkles
on my face

sworn in the memory
of my language

swimming in the blood
of my grandchildren

Secwepemc-ke

Secwepemc-ke: I am Shuswap

The Hide-Tanner's Odyssey

hide scraper in hand
he drags calluses over
a dead-weight skin slumped on
a smooth pole, singing wet songs

carcass flinging decayed-flesh
scent into the heat of Indian Summer

the blood-soaked hair drips, drips
the medicine towards earth
disappears
like long-gone bones

never remembered
never known

the hair is cropped from the skin
stretched on the rack
and scraped until
every membrane is dry

this is the life of an Indian

The Hide-Tanner's Pole

the hide-tanner's pole is sleek
sanded to silk-wooden skin

count the rings of life
it lived

the skin of a buck the hunter saw die
offers future warmth

soaked to the membrane and dripping
the lifeless skin wraps around the pole

digging into it
he scrapes off the remnants of flesh

tears at the fur
humming an ancestral song

at the Feast to Honour the Dead, we pray
to the pole, the buck and the dust

of grandmothers who dreamed
our doings into living form

The Highway of Tears

women bent over bones
murmuring the names of those killed
along the Highway of Tears

conscience awakens in the crow of night
lurid dreams expel the myth
that keeps lights on in the dark

lies are for hiding things
think about Bundy and the Green Mountain executioner
and slaughter pits along isolated roads

knowing "this-is-just-one-less-native-bitch" mentality
knowing the RCMP will never do the right thing
survivors chant words in solidarity

the numbers keep climbing toward heaven
fists bludgeon on concrete walls
gnaw on rosaries and spit out names

the nation fights back the lumps in throats
wards off strangers who look at daughters
turn inward thinking we are at fault

helplessly, we sing Tea Dance songs
calling on the forerunners
to finally bring our women home

Shanks and Tattoo Guns

the whites of the eyes tattooed
in red and blue prison inks see
the human condition as opaque

there are no corners on wild flowers
to fantasize about
nor to call into question wild scents

the streets are full
of potential residents
torn from the place called home

in the big house, jellybean arguments turn deadly
with shanks and tattoo guns in hand
life is a fragile story waiting to be told

when the ink turns to tears . . .

Doomed

there's a bullet
with my name on it

a dog tag dangling
from a pit bull's neck

hatred stands alone
at sweaty gun point

the dogs bark
the grass bends

a black eye winks away
shadows in eyes

afraid of the sun
afraid of the dog within

fight or flight are options
and cowards are real

take me down
take me down

Elements of Novel Study

stimulation is sought
conjuring the plot, the gossip, the exploration
worthy of examination

conflicts are necessary
the intensity, the lashing of the tongue
awakens sensibility and steers resolution

the seeker searches comfort
avoiding the wolf's teeth
the story line unfolds

obstacles rip open the protagonist's motives
man against man, man versus nature, man versus evil
the antagonist conceives a hero

conflicts lurk in the belly of the shark
an ocean of turbulence opens
builds hurricanes in the eyes

emotional splinters puncture intent
juxtapositions baffle
contemplation is mundane

discovery of the human condition is bent
on survival
drawing out new stories

what we learn
what we share
the elements of life

Shame

a cowardly baby
shame jammed inside
witnessing women beaten
dragged down, torn apart

he is weak
I am weak

a terrified child
peeking around corners
puking up the lump in his throat
knowing that brutality becomes legacy

he is tearful
I am tearful

a useless man
gutless with pen and paper in hand
unable to scrawl words
strong enough to halt subjugation

he is guilty
I am guilty

a god-fearing crippled old man
stuffing his heart full of profound
excuses to mask
self-loathing, self-pity, self-doubt

he is compelled
I am compelled

the signatory to this document
testifying to the principles
of our mothers, our sisters
our women

STOP! before you go any further

John Wayne

cowboy poets are romantic illusionists
cling-clanging poems Custer style
spouting lyrics bow-legged across stages
dry pumping John Wayne hard-ons
twanging in all the natural places

driving the team with rhythm and rhyme
Yankee-doodling with black microphones in hand
yodeling yippy-yi yay, yippy-yi yoh
crooning southern sweet words across airwaves
reining in the audience from a full gallop forward

each poem kicks out bucking-horse metaphors
rendering flushed faces on saggy-skinned gals
drop-mouthed and lip-stick blurred
running to washrooms sniggering awkwardly
as the toilets twirl horse shit all the way down to the NFR

hill-billy limericks stuff the heart full of wind-swept words
bulging out jugulars
when they splatter barnyard poetics on set
like cattle pissing down on flat rocks on hot summer days
· bringing forth quixotic redneck notions

redneck reality or redneck illusion is tough
to reckon with — never mind that
delusion is the business of sonnets
when you're born a cowboy poet
meant to live a John Wayne life

Dime Store

from the dingy junk-strewn streets
amid industrial towers hemorrhaging
soot along graffiti-filled walls
Jane Doe swaggers pigeon-toed in stilettos
strutting straight on towards John's revving motor
crushing needles
fulfilling fantasies

Jane knows every John
cruising by slowly in suit and tie
whips and leather rubbing his cock
eye-balling her pathway to the dime store
fantasizing warm places

he cries in his beer
caters to his stay-at-home princess
takes the kids to soccer
attends parent-teacher interviews
shows up for work on time
but when the family is gone
sweeping streets is home

Jane knows the silent knife
that could slit her throat
with his cock the bullet
stuffing her full of wrath
pounding out the music the tyrant dances to

on lonely nights, when the family is gone
his blood pumps
from mild to wild
a wallet full of tens
a mind dizzy with disbelief
the fix is turning off the key

deep within, she knows
she is more transparent
than the wife he hides at home

A Child of Our Own

a man's selfish pleasure often overpowers
reliability and responsibility

pride with shameless intent

it is pretentious conversation
for the boys on Sunday morning

never putting two and two together

though the fling was lopsided perfection
when the moon laced the curtains

the attitude that followed was not

a pregnancy was unforeseen
cause for denial

the boy's damage was done

so when the realization becomes
a child growing within sacredness

the flight overrides the fight for fatherhood

disowning his own is knowing
that some men are not man enough

to do the things that fathers should

and what results is a nameless child
bent on hate

wondering who the father is

Secret Weapon

internalized craziness
twists and muzzles the brain
agonizes the body
like a Picasso or a Goya's
interpretation of life
when death seems the only option

sensible words are hard to come by
don't ask
don't say
don't tell
the story of suicide or murder or rape
or the origin of one's sexuality —
because secrets are weapons to die for

and the bone-yard men wait
for another to dream death

– thunderstorms –

Thunderstorms

I love thunderstorms
rain on the tin roof at midnight
your breath
my breath
hearts in our rib cages pounding
breathless and blind
as lips compel lips
the scent of the earth
when the rain begins

I am drawn in by the silk sheets
the puddles of fresh rain
your skin
my skin
the bending of limbs
leaves belly-dancing
as the wind shifts songs
the colour of night
when the rain begins

it is meant to be this way
you
me
thunderstorms

Naropa Days

I remember you
from the Naropa days

young poets bogged down
in a ditch of poetic meditation

dazzled by Ginsberg's aesthetics
pink and blue poems blossomed from lust

soaked in the scent of wet pavement
after a Rocky Mountain rain

felt deep the black boulder
wedged between our hearts and skin

craving a life
that could never be

my carpenter's eye was clouded then
but I was there in '88

Faith

my prayers are embedded
in an old cracked rosary strewn
with black lies chained
to a tarnished crucifix

I swore I could heal
your tormented heart
but my real words hide
in private places

my prayers wait to voyage
to the outer limits of my skin
when my eyes give birth
to the thunder beings sleeping within

it is then they will speak stories
of the sun-bleached blade we found
above the wet earth
with the exposed bone piles

my soul is cool now
like those skeletons
waiting for a healing song
to call us home

Grandchildren

grandchildren are full
of endless questions

"Grandpa, how did the bear walk on you?"
"How did the sun set on your arm?"
"Where is the moon, when it is snowing?"

my answers are never the same
and I forget how I've answered them before

"It is night time," I say.
"Close your eyes and go to sleep."
"But Grandpa, you know I always sleep with my eyes open."

grandchildren see the world in full colour
and taste the sound of every word they are told

Inside Out

no one can love
without grief
there is
some worth
in turning the other cheek
but more
in turning the self
inside out
crawling
back and forth
pushing the fist
through the skin
groping at the heart
willing to yank it out
because grief is
misunderstood
and so is
love

Yours

the day the skies sweat rain
I undressed you in a bundle of clover
in the open fields of possibilities

anticipating what was to come
I sank into you
staring into your soul's skylight

my fingers fluttered a hummingbird dance
over the fullness of your breasts, your belly
as the rain quickened skin scents

the ride to the valley below
was the Moon devouring Earth
as you guided me to your sacredness

from that moment to this day
when the memory became etched in this poem
I have been yours

Creative Prerequisites

you impressed me with cornflakes
believed in god just in case
we had to grow old together
bravery is something
we are born with

seeking happiness is full of cheap surprises
unexpected delights at breakfast
cemeteries in my mind
flowers in dark places

the coffee sits by the cereal bowl
and I am thirsty
and starving

Dangerous Words: The Trio

1 — ARCHIBALD (GREY OWL)

Pauline, angel, hear these words:

I speak from the grave
no longer a clerk in a lumberyard

I am the younger blood of Duncan
the brother who fills my spirit with life

I am the man stifled by my upbringing
abandoned by my mother, despised by my father, the drunkard

I am imprisoned with fear
terrified of letting go

I carry double-bladed knives in my body
to protect the man hiding beneath the child

I paddle my way to love
believing you and I are "pilgrims of the wild"

yet I am horrified
to release the butterflies within

I escape to Toronto convinced by an angel with
soft teeth whispering dangerous words

I see her in the ripples of Lake Huron
she is shrouded by silk black wings caressing her desperation

I return to the bush-lands in northern Ontario
lie sexless on wild rose petals and thorns beside Angele

I rattle prayers over swamp tea the next morning with Duncan
while she tangles quaint discussions with those she despises

I savour the taste of my brother and roses
thinking of the love waiting at the periphery

I remember songs on the tips of my fingers
and pull a cigarette from behind my ear, reminiscing

I cling to the protective pouch hanging around my neck
hum a holy song hoping it will reach lands across the ocean

I sense my own mother, Kittie, burrowing below my skin
a ghostly sorrow stopping my growth

I curse because of her fork-tongued torture
the crippling she has bestowed upon me

Pauline, because of her, I seek to embrace true love
God hands it to me by bow and arrow, but then

I scream the unacceptable
hiding in the shadow of my angel's wings

I run to the "devil in deerskins"
fantasize I am the "red Indian"

I stop the wind from raising the hairs on my arms
because I realize I am better in the wild than I am in love

I build wigwams beneath my skin
yet secretly want the inside to burst of body heat

I transport blue stones and give jade knives to Duncan
because I know no other way to ask for his help, yet

I am so afraid to look him in the eye
does this means death or life?

I know your power to hate him
is less than mine

I rub your imaginary aches, run to get afternoon tea
turn down invitations of reality for you, Pauline

I offer my lumberyard body to the brown-skinned girls
as servant in each living moment I am present, but

I deprive all of you of my masculine prime
this is my power

I know angels lose divine beauty
when they desire control instead of freedom, and

I know when this happens, they fall
from heaven never to return to the "tales of an empty cabin"

I recall everything
step by step, I move to Riding Mountain Park

I am compelled to be near the Indians
in a wildernesses of my own making, to remember

I ink tattoos on my arms, around my neck to tell stories
the demon and the angel, the prison and the escape

I never wash the sweat of Duncan from my body
he protects me from mother; I know you smell him on me

I play on this because you, my sweet Pauline, are afraid of him
yet I know you churn poison to rub into his pores

I stare stone-faced out of windows waiting for my brother
but the nights are long — I wait at the edge of the bone-yard

2 — PAULINE

Archibald, I am Pauline, the angel in the dark rooms
at Chiefswood although the public claims otherwise

I believe they hide in their own darkness, musing therein
since by birth, they have made me a British ward

but I have tricks and magic
the beauty and exotic Native lulling in didactic tones

I can command and control every wish, every desire
every movement on the parts of my tongue where mothers live

I fantasize pulsing groins, as does your brother, Duncan
but I loathe the woman who has given birth to him, as I do him

I am a mismatch for him
I am power, I have the blood of Indian women in me

I see you are everything
he is not

I call on the ancestors at dreamtime for a vision
they show me the Canadian despot, the scoundrel

I place porcupine quills in the tender parts of my body
so that the destructiveness may repulse him but awaken others

I know this as a skill, the magic-making
the control mechanisms for love in the right pitch

I can destroy the mother who lurks within you
knowing that I am childless, but mother enough to replace her

I am years wiser and ahead of you, I am Indian woman
and I know the weaknesses of men forty times over

I have slept with them all, their thoughts, their weaknesses
I have learned that a woman goes for the soul, not the heart

I can easily shatter those shields protecting a man's heart
make tears glisten on warrior blades, their soul the prize

I am the rediscovered feminist, emphasizing style
an artifact rendered as the first Canadian woman

I will not let you forget "A Cry from an Indian Wife"
from the Battle at Cutknife Creek

I lip "The Song My Paddle Sings"
thinking of you, thinking of Riel, thinking of them all

I know Duncan does not rate me as the real thing, but
he explores the edge of my bed, smelling the moss

I move closer to find my love — roam the mountains
finger dancing along the ridges of my body

I hear soft violins moaning deep within like those in Verona
where Romeo and Juliet were doves cooing desperation

I discover ecstasy burning on my lips, my thighs
are Moses' burning bush needing the gush of wetness

I am quick to sizzle the intertwining of rage and despair
since you lie dormant near Lake Winnipeg, northern and cold

I remind myself hissing, that angels construct heaven
knowing that men, like you, allow the rivers to run dry

I realize that my magic is useless with you
but my aging body and active mind are relentless

I endlessly seek the coy advice of Tarot cards
reading into the details of my maneuvers

I coil the sweetness of the serpent's breath
on the bitter part of my tongue, vibrating commands

I summon you to deliver or I will end my life
and since you are a child, you obey jokingly

I lie upon my velvet bedding like my sister, Cleopatra,
preserved in a house museum, my breasts burning of cancer

I close the lily-lace curtains draped in tribal costumes
lash out with meaningless tasks to appease my disappointments

I appeal to Duncan's chambers, for he is your equal
and while the sweat drips off the hairs on his chest

I whisper, "Grey Owl
can you see me laid across forests, plains and mountains?"

my secrets are butterflies fluttering in his anger
I know my end is near — will you come with me, Grey Owl?

3 — DUNCAN CAMPBELL SCOTT

Pauline, I adore you, my angel, the other I am not,
our lives will be one as with the Onondaga Madonna

I have built the Canadian empire awaiting your arrival
parliaments scoping a path to heaven, all for your pagan ways

I wander the rooms peering south and west and north and east
anxious for the moment the canoes come, delivering you to me

I want the blood of all Indian women
opened at the arteries, drained of their ancestors

I want their sons hung on meat hooks
their flesh to be preserved as thought only

I want Canada whitewashed
its museums dotted with Indian corpses

I want extermination policies
bulging from the eyes of heirs yet to come

I earthquake tremble with excitement
my younger brother, Grey Owl, stands by my side

I love him, like no other can, as he does me,
for I am familiar with the absolute oneness of brothers

I am the older, and so I wrap my heavenly arms around him
protecting him from hideous nightmares

I swirl within, for my purpose is evident
he is my purpose, I give him purpose as he does me

I discharge sweat in the palms of my hands
dampening the whetstone I bring everywhere

I sharpen my weapons, my words, my desires
so that my stone structures are forever a fortress

I will protect him as I do you, sweet Pauline
for I am the federal civil servant territorial

I forge assimilation policies
mapping trails of hatred from coast to coast for eternity

"I want to get rid of the Indian problem
until there is not one single Indian in Canada"

I beg you, sweet Pauline
do not eclipse my role in history

I desire to stamp my dream within the Canadian psyche
and build a legacy worthy to leave my beloved wards

I am the pianist, the poet, the prose writer
but know that my love is powerful enough for you as well

I see you, oh Pauline
I see all of you: the pink mornings and orange evenings

I also recognize the blackness of nights without moon
shining in your eyes

I imagine the brilliance of day, I want it:
roses petals slow dancing for the sun, carcasses dangling

I understand the language of natural heat
swimming below the sun, above the earth

I am solid with the power of words
the blood of my mother dampening my tongue

I sculpt my words, for you my sweet, a voice like yours
making the wind shake life into the leaves lodged in my throat

I am ablaze throughout my body, my skin sizzles to my bone
what has happened to me?

I call on you: an arrow song for my ear, to speak into my soul
but you conjure magic at the very windows where I have stood

I await the outcome as still morning unveils shadows
climbing stonewalls for my enlightenment

I see your eyes exploring my brother
undressing him, enslaving him, entrapping him

I know he is loyal to me
and will not deceive the origin of his virtue

I am naked before you
handsome atop your angelic body

I whisper "close your eyes"
death waits at the doors of hell for you, lovely Pauline.

I will spare Archibald
for we are the same

Venus and the Rez Lover Boy

oh the rez boy knows
beauty is only cock deep

he's seen it on tv while gawking at Venus
as Ms. Lopez flashed her silky sleek pathway
all the way to the Latina beaver pond

and the rez boys chit-chattered bug-eyed
about the effects and canyons of good hunting
.30-30s loaded and ready to discharge
erupting lava bullets from the barrels
gushing enough to soak buck-berry bushes
and buzzing the boys into raw rez buck-fever

like all boys, the rez boy bragged about imaginary conquests
new-moon eyes glimmered at the Goddess of Love
lying atop a sheet of fir boughs
naked and dazzling
legs and toes pointing east to west
tongue circling the twirling planets
high speed belly dancing when heaven touched earth

the arousal was stunning, he boasted
as he watched spiders crawling in her veins
webbing their bodies into godly erotica
sparking intensity with his he-bee gee-bee moves
he was so proud as her fingertips ripped into bark
tearing off flesh
sucking on the sap
screaming out his big daddy reservation name

for a moment, Apollo was *Koyoti*
bullet proof, hedonistic and accomplished
sending tremors that rumbled the skies
causing a sea of foam to flood the undergrowth

finally, the climax came
and the rez boy turned off the tv

If I

if I were to catch you smiling
I could bring you back
from the dead, like me

if I were to glide my fingers
along the silhouette of your face
touching that smile
wiping that tear
your life would begin, like mine

if I were to guide you
to the safety of what lives deep inside
and release the butterflies craving freedom
bringing on that smile
the excursion of your love story would begin, and be ours

if I were to . . .

Vail

we explored Colorado's Vail
shimmering aspens exposed yellow on the mountainsides
mist seeped into mountain pores like joyful tears
and I harmonized "I'm your southern man"

ancient rock faces stared down
reminding us that beyond ourselves
there is a magnitude in life
older than our history

winter was not so far off, and so
an avalanche of hearts was ready
to rumble down slopes
colliding fervently before the Old Ones

my heaving force raced up and down my spine
as you leaned back against still-born dreams
and now I overflow with thoughts of you
even after all of those years leaving Colorado

The Art of Dialing

lover-boy compelled
to resurrect dead love
scrolled in Blackberry numbers

finger flips the phone directory
swooping memory's archives
stuffing his soul full of relentless flutters

anticipation full of compulsion
reaching for our song — a saxophone-droning song
the last supper, the last night, the last name

he thought it was all imprinted
on paths where strawberries were strewn
on silk sheets and in telephone logs

so clear were the sounds of love
smashing rocks to sand
drifting in artistic dialing like art on canvas

ring, ring, ring
the live-wires erect, heart full of enthusiasm
but then a stranger answers

Koyoti Rain

warm skin and a setting moon
tell the story of pumping hearts

it is the surrender of blood and desires
silken words spun in cocoons

carried as the wind's truth to dry people
waiting for the *Koyoti* rain to fall tenderly

wild sunflowers heard the loon's song
and the roots of silence flourish

Koyoti Sky Story

he scaled
music upon her thighs
koyoti-moaning notes

looking up, she saw airplanes
ripping clouds
and clenched a bundle of clover

he faced earth
wanting mountains to bleed streams
to hear the wings of whiskey jacks flying overhead

she lay upon her back
thinking of heaven
and what it would be like to live

and when the music stopped
life began for the both of them
he found purpose then

she whispered "don't cry. we are alive."

Honey Talk

all that honey talk was garble
wrap-the-fingers-around-the-neck
breath-taking jargon
dreamed up on frigid nights

o sweet baby
my skin is beneath your fingertips
my throat is wet huffing the doghouse blues
as you pant your way to another love

it was all new-moon action
burgundy fluid calling gravity home
the pillows are stained, the windows are bleeding condensation
and morning would not come too soon

o sweet baby
my scent is on your hands
my mind is fat with your image
as you sand my fragrance into the flesh of another guy

all that honey talk was blocked in
put-another-log-on-the-fire
tea-sipping memories
dreamed up on frigid nights

Falling Snow

the furnace shuttles along constantly
the snow falls in peaceful silence
the moon is south right now
here in the north daylight is rare these days

I think about friends as Christmas nears
Janet, Richard, Brian, even Chris
what are they doing at this moment?
the winter draws out thoughts on long days

early winter is an enchanted time
scents of summer pine seem long forgotten
as is the taste of saskatoons after a summer rain
moments in falling snow

Dancing Silly

I dance silly for you
when the evening sky
turns an oyster grey
and night approaches

my naked feet slide side to side
promising Paso Doble
when the scent of the moon
fills heaven

my hands double-beat the sound
of trumpets swelling the heart with laughter
as you giggle contentment
watching me

the rhythms beckon you
to love me as you once did
with my Northern Man song
I dance silly

and when my callused feet
touch yours
our journey will be clear
silly as it may be

ABOUT THE AUTHOR

Garry Gottfriedson, from the Secwepemc Nation (Shuswap), was born, raised and lives in Kamloops, BC. He holds a masters of education from Simon Fraser University and has studied Creative Writing at the Naropa Institute in Boulder, Colorado. He currently works as the principal at the Sk'elep School of Excellence in Kamloops, BC. His published works include: *100 Years of Contact* (SCES, 1990); *In Honour of Our Grandmothers* (Theytus, 1994); *Glass Tepee* (Thistledown, 2002) nominated for First People's Publishing Award 2004; *Painted Pony* (Partners in Publishing, 2005); *Whiskey Bullets* (Ronsdale, 2006), the Anskohk Aboriginal Award Finalist; *Skin Like Mine* (Ronsdale, 2010), shortlisted for Canadian Author's Literary Award for Poetry 2011; and *Jimmy Tames Horses* (Kegedonce, 2012). His works have been anthologized both nationally and internationally. He has read from his work in Canada, the USA, Europe and Asia.